Brampton Poets 2019

Anthology

Print ISBN 978-1-9996676-4-1

Dedication

This collection of poetry is dedicated to the memory of Gilbert Hutchinson, erudite, ornithologist, bookworm and poet. From the genesis of the group until his death in 2017, Gilbert was an enthusiastic member and supporter of our activities. Indeed, without his early expression of interest, the group may never have come into existence.

Brampton Poets 2019

CONTENTS

David Hurd

Ruth Kershaw

John S Langley

Stuart Turner

Space for poems of your own

Acknowledgements

Our thanks are due to the *Cottage Coffee community* for the financial assistance that made this anthology possible and to Aidan Meehan for permission to use the illustrations (for which he retains the Copyright).

Brampton Poets 2019

Preface

Brampton Poets is a name assumed by a group of people who meet monthly in the Community Centre in Brampton. The group was born out of a Poetry Breakfast event in the Theatre by the Lake in Keswick in 2016, under the umbrella of Words by the Water, at which people were invited to gather for breakfast and to read poetry: their own or that of others.

Ena and Gilbert Hutchinson, Brampton residents, took the concept back to Brampton, contacted a number of acquaintances whom they knew to be interested in poetry and suggested adopting the same format on a monthly basis.

The group meets at 10 a.m. on the first Thursday of every month, enjoys breakfast and chat for half an hour, then reads poetry for a period of 45 minutes to an hour.

The idea of this anthology was prompted by the meetings of the group. Some of the members who write poetry have contributed samples of their work with the intention of sharing their creations with a wider public.

Brampton Poets 2019

The Poets

David Bamford

David Bamford came to live in Lanercost in 2010 after having worked in education in South America for 22 out of the previous 25 years. He returned to UK to retire, but soon found himself working part time at Austin Friars School in Carlisle, teaching Spanish, until they ran out of hours for him. Shortly after retiring for the second time, he was offered a few hours teaching French at Hayton C of E Primary School, which he loves.

David has had a love of poetry for as long as he can remember and numbers poets among his forebears. He is also a Reader in the Church of England, an active participant in theatrical activities and an inveterate writer of letters to the Cumberland News.

He sees poetry as a form or written expression that captures a moment of inspiration and fixes it as a kind of epiphany (and he hopes that doesn't sound too pompous!)

Lorna Burnhams

Lorna Burnhams was born in the West Midlands to a Northern Irish father and a Black Country mother. She has worked in several occupations, including teaching. Throughout her life she has lived in various parts of the UK from Devon to Durham in both urban and rural landscapes.

Early in life Lorna's older sisters introduced her to poetry, encouraging her to both read and write poems. This opened up a world of endless possibilities. In later life she has returned to writing poetry. Her subject matter is varied, but she has a particular interest in identity and memory.

David Hurd

David Hurd was born in 1940 and lived for the first ten years of his life in Scarborough. He then lived for five years in Wetheral. At the age of fifteen he joined the army and trained as a cartographic draughtsman. He served twenty years in the army before being made redundant.

David worked at Bartholemew's in Edinburgh, then at Metal Box in Carlisle. He then worked for a small reproduction company, doing art and film work for various printers until he was made redundant again at 55.

He then spent four years at the Cumbria College of Art and now produces three-dimensional creations using clay, welded metal and fibreglass, carved wood and stone. He also spends more time writing poetry, to which he was first alerted before leaving Irthing Vale school.

The poems in this collection were written while David was in Singapore.

Ruth Kershaw

Ruth has lived in Brampton for 50 years. Born in Rochdale, but, due to her father's promotions on the railway, found herself in Halifax by the time she was 10. Here she stayed until she had gained School Certificate. Now at the northern end of the chain, Ruth thinks of herself as a Pennine woman and revels in their wildness. She has walked the Pennine Way.

A long period of bedrest (age 6/rheumatic fever) gave time to indulge in Arthur Mee's encyclopedia, the Poetry and Natural History sections laying foundation for lifelong interests.

She is indebted to her English teacher for encouraging her to write essays but did not venture into poetry until 2013 when she enjoyed a Poetry Course at Stones Barn led by Ian Duhig. Immediately `hooked' she has attended 2 more of the same.

A retired Methodist Minister, she finds poems easier than sermons.

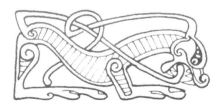

John S Langley

John Langley was born and raised in the North East of England and has two brothers, three sons and only one wife.

After qualifying as a Chemical Engineer he was lucky enough to work around the world on various projects before moving into Consultancy and finally becoming his own Company.

He has enjoyed writing creatively all his life, a trait that was not always appreciated whilst at school, but the disciplines of Technical Report writing put something of a dampener on this for about 30 years.

Now settled back in the North he has time to write with freedom and experimentation and has even built up enough courage to admit to being an Author and a Poet.

Stuart Turner

Stuart Turner was born on 7th May 1942 in
Newcastle and spent his childhood in Consett,
a steel town in County Durham (the Steel
Works closed in 1980). He belongs very much
to the Christian family and the upholding of
Christian traditions. He attended Annfield
Plain Secondary Modern School and
was introduced to Literature, in particular, by
his Headmaster, who was a brilliant man with
the iconic name of W.E.Gladstone.

He started writing poetry in1962 after he
joined the Royal Air Force and concentrated
more specifically on this after the millennium
in 2000 when he had more time after raising a
family. He has engaged in both verse and
prose and his writing usually focuses on a
mixture of nature and human interaction.

The Poems

David Bamford

Pilgrimage

Putting one foot in front of the other
In tune with my surroundings and myself
Longing for the goal that draws me on.
God's joy in my heart, and a song
Ringing out to nature,
In adoration of Him who
Made it all for my delight,
And us in His image and to do His Will.
God wills and we obey
Eternally.

Passage of Winter

The last languid crow-flight of autumn,
the cawing call,
a plangent, fading echo on the wind.
Finger-ended wings spread,
a silhouette of black against the grey.

Skeletal-branching trees,
grey against the bleakness.
Fields of curry-comb stubble,
beige against the brown,
a sepia landscape, motionless
below the level of the scything breeze,
but cold, lifeless.

Sheep huddled in sodden pasture,
cattle motionless in mud.
Troughs stand in murky liquid mirrors.
Life suspended, dormant.

In churchyards, forebears sleep,
undisturbed and undisturbing,
while, by a drunken tombstone,
a bunch of snowdrops shyly peeps.
The final flower of winter,
or herald of a coming spring?

Somnambulist

When I was a child, I used to walk in my sleep.
It never bothered me. – Well, it wouldn't. I
wasn't aware of it. My parents told me that they
once stopped me as I was about to open a door
that led from the landing onto a balcony. I
eventually grew out of it, but the memory of
being told that I had this habit has stayed with
me, and I find it intriguing.

I watch you walking,
cushioned within the cocoon
of your unconscious security.
Unwavering,
guided by an unknown sense of purpose,
gliding through the darkness.
Your lips move,
muttering unheard, unheeded sounds.
You wander from your bedroom,
hair awry,
nightdress fluttering in an unfelt breeze.
Your eyes, unseeing, yet are open.
A fragile smile quivers at the corners of your
mouth.
Light furrows plough across your brow.
You go to cross the landing,
pause, and change direction,
stop before the picture of a landscape,
raise a hand, caress it, smile,

comb your fingers through your hair,
fidget, shrug your shoulders.
'Hm!' a little laugh.
'Hm, hm!' a giggle,
childlike in its innocence.
Dilated pupils show a sign
-   of fear? Concern?
'Where am I?' they seem to say.
Mind made up,
you move again,
enter the bedroom, close the door.
The latch clicks shut
and bedsprings creak.
Then . . .
Silence.

St Mary's Church, Lindisfarne, Trinity Sunday 2017

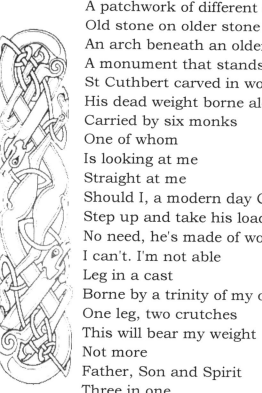

Surroundings unadorned, majestic
Eloquent in their silence
A patchwork of different stone
Old stone on older stone
An arch beneath an older arch
A monument that stands
St Cuthbert carved in wood
His dead weight borne aloft
Carried by six monks
One of whom
Is looking at me
Straight at me
Should I, a modern day Cyrenean,
Step up and take his load?
No need, he's made of wood
I can't. I'm not able
Leg in a cast
Borne by a trinity of my own
One leg, two crutches
This will bear my weight
Not more
Father, Son and Spirit
Three in one
'not a scientific riddle to be puzzled out
A life to which we're drawn by name.'

The preacher's words not mine
Three in one
An ancient building
A house of prayer
A place of worship
Voices raised aloft
In praise and veneration
Holy Trinity
I can neither understand you
Nor explain you
Yet I will worship you
In spirit and, I hope,
In truth.

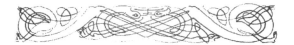

New Year, new week

Written on 1st January 2018

Twenty eighteen began on a Monday
New Year, new week.
Old year, battered, beaten,
cracked, fracked,
terrorist attacked.
Trump dumped tweets upon the world,
ill-considered, unthinking.
A profusion of confusion,
illusion and delusion.
Brexit wrecks it,
Politicians hex it,
while we live our lives as best we can.

The year rolls out. It's gone
The world rolls on. Still here.
What's behind is over,
What's before is undefined.
May May be cast ere the may be out,
or may she stay and tough it out,
Beset, besieged, beleaguered?

New week, New Year.
Begin again,
start anew.
Find hope in something,
in ourselves, outside,
or bigger than ourselves?

There must be hope in something.
Maybe in Prince Harry's grin,
or in the sparkle
that is seen to shine from Meghan Markle.
These could bring a spark of joy
to many.
Look for the bright side, and look on it.
See the good in others.
Celebrate it, shout it to the world.
Make the most of every chance.
New week, New Year.
Rejoice. Begin again.

Solway

The first steps on a walk along the Hadrian's
Wall path from west to east

From Bowness, through the arch
into a Narnia of my own.
What lies beyond?
Miles of river estuary
flowing slowly, a mobile mass of chocolate milk
flecked with white marshmallow foam,
past this crumb on the tongue
of Cumbria's northern coast.

Myself, the massive sky for company.
To the north, Dumfries and Galloway,
etched hard and sharp as uncut jewels.
Green, purple, brown against the blue.
Wind turbines, slim white pencils,
glisten in the winter's sun.

Free, untied from time amid this space,
I shout for joy.
The sound plucked by the wind
and carried off,
lost in the immensity
of the river's kingdom,
drowned by the wailing of the gulls.

Sheep have wandered from the pasture
through the fence
to where the grass is, doubtless, greener,
to graze.
They stare at me in curious quizzicality,
ruminating, wary, teeth grinding sideways.
Then they bolt.
Of course, I'm not their shepherd,
they don't know me. They don't trust me.
I'm an alien to them.

But one.
She stands her ground, defiant.
Her eyes say 'I'm not scared of you.
You're on my patch.
Don't ask me to budge.'
She's right. I'm passing through,
a moving dot along the path
where Roman legions tramped,
beneath the empire's northern sky,
where the river Solway flows
endlessly towards the Irish sea.

Thin Place

A 'thin place' is a place where, apparently, the space between earth and heaven (the veil) is very slender and where one can sense the presence of the Divine. A number of these are evident, though not by that name, in the Bible and in narrated encounters between God and human beings. Think of Noah and the instructions given to him for the building of the Ark, Jacob and his dream of a ladder reaching between earth and heaven, Moses and the burning bush, Elijah, fleeing from the wrath of King Ahab, hiding in a cave in Hebron and hearing the 'still small voice' of God, the baptism of Jesus, his transfiguration, St John and the revelation received on the Island of Patmos. There are many.
In April 2017, I travelled round part of the Republic of Ireland, visiting listed 'thin places' and enjoying the peace to be found in them.

A vast landscape,
ground meeting sky, heaven touching earth.
A thin place where I enjoy my solitude,
not lonely, though alone.

Hills sweep to the horizon, turning blue,
dotted with groves of trees.

Sheep, cattle, little toys standing on an endless
eiderdown of green.
Birds, scraps of paper in the wind,
sweep, career, turn, swivel, corkscrew,
riding gusts and currents.

Somewhere above, an aeroplane
roars faintly on its way to somewhere,
I know not where
and I don't care.
My journey's here,
for now.

Alone. A figure in a landscape.
Nothing to no one. No one knows I'm here.
I crept out early, in the dawn's pink light,
to walk to where I've come.
In the stillness, in the thinness,
the earth below, heaven above.
I'm squeezed between the two.
'Nearer, my God, to Thee.'

Lonlay l'Abbaye

In the very hot July of 2018, my wife and I spent a week in the little Normandy town of Lonlay l'Abbaye. We rented a renovated cobbler's cottage and enjoyed a week of utter tranquility.

In the heat of a July afternoon
nothing stirs
and time stands still.
No movement in the square,
no motion in the air.
The birds are silent in the trees,
Not a whisper, no breath of breeze.
It's Monday; shops are closed, the cafe's shut.
Life seems suspended,
floating motionless, and yet,
the clock on the tower of the ancient church
strikes the hour,
then the quarter,
then the half,
then three quarters
and another hour.
It's too hot to move,
yet time moves on,
making mockery of the stillness.
Inexorable, ineluctable,
like action in a tragedy
moving to its climax.
We are fixed, in the July heat not moving,

yet constrained by time's treadmill
to a movement that will not be stopped.
The clock moves on
and strikes another quarter,
then the half
and then three quarters,
and then another hour.
Our mortality won't stop it.
We may be dead, or gone,
but hours, quarters, halves, three-quarters,
other hours
will still strike on.

Cappuccino

*One day, with time to spare, when I was waiting
to meet my wife in Carlisle, I called into a café
and ordered a cappuccino, not a form of coffee
that I often drink. I enjoyed it so much that I
wrote the following, which I posted on
TripAdvisor and sent to the Cumberland News.
Much to my surprise, the newspaper published
it.*

This afternoon,
I ordered a cappuccino.
Regular,
club card duly tendered.

The barista
(isn't that what they're called?)
swiped the card and smiled.
"You can have a free coffee today,"
she said (they always add 'today'.
Not 'tomorrow,' not 'next week.')
"Would you like a large one, as it's free?"
"No, thank you," I replied, and wondered
What she would have thought
If I'd said, "not today,"?
But I don't think that fast. In any case,
it might seem rude.

Instead, I smiled and thanked her.
She said she'd take it
to my table.
She did. She also took my book.
She must have seen
that I was lame
and had a crutch.
Kindness personified.
I thanked her again,
told her she was very kind.

I took a sip.
Sweet taste of powdered chocolate
on lips and tongue.
She hadn't asked me if I wanted it.
Why do they do that?
Without chocolate,
surely,
it's not a cappuccino.
Foam. Luxuriant, thick and white
as a swan's down duvet.
Then the hot and bitter stab
of coffee.

THAT's a cappuccino.
The best I've ever tasted.

Epitaph?

When I am dead,
what will be said of me?
Will those I wronged forgive me,
as I forgive
those who've done me wrong?
Will those I've loved forget me
and get on with their lives,
glossing over faults?
Will I be sent away
with words of gratitude
or strings of platitude?
With what attitudes
will those who knew me think of me?
Will they condemn me
when my body turns to ash
and my dust returns to dust?
Will they dismiss my faults,
airbrush my blemishes,
inflating those poor virtues
which I strove in vain to show?
Will it matter what they say
or what they think
when I am gone?
I will have lived a life,
one among a myriad others.
We occupy a space on earth.
It closes when we go,
as if we never were,
and yet

I tried to live, to love, to give.
Was I received?
I'll never know.
And, in the end,
it will not matter
when I am dead.

Lorna Burnhams

Home

Here tonight in this city of flimsy tents,
Where the cold seeps inside with deadly ease,
They know a home can be as fragile as a small
    songbird's nest.
It can be broken open by bombs or burnt to the
    ground,
Or simply left in fear.
But still the hope of that abandoned place,
Creates a longing that is stronger now
And still they are afraid.
It is too late...
For them to sit and watch the children play out
    in the sunlit courtyard.
Or see the young ones creep into the kitchen,
Lured by the sweet smell of date cookies baking
    for Eid.
Too late to chop fresh parsley and stir the spices
    into the meatballs bubbling on the stove.
It is too late to place those treasured coffee cups
Carefully on the copper tray for the expected
    guests. Where are they now?
So late...
Too late to hear the local muezzin call for
    evening prayers from the minaret.
Where is he now? No one knows. His wife has
    not heard from him in a year.

Way too late to lie back against the cushions
  piled upon the couch,
And feel the gentle weight of a new baby warm
  against their arm.
That was long ago and he has gone to fight for
  freedom. They don't know where.
They only know he isn't here in this cold tent
  with them,
Maybe if he was, it would seem a little nearer
  home.

The Bell

Always afraid of the tolling bell
I remember my fear when the old king died,
Five and frightened I knew so well
If a king could die then so could a child.

I felt the warmth of my sisters' hands.
I was rich in sisters – we were three,
All my fears soon were left behind
They were there to soothe and comfort me.

Caught in the alchemy of chance and time
Those shielding arms are cold and still.
It is they who are long left behind
Leaving me alone to face the bell.

Crows

Waddling out of the dark wood on black, scaly
    feet come the crows.
If eagles are the kings of the birds,
then these harbingers of danger are the
    ruffians:
A ragged mob stealing eggs and naked
    nestlings.
Riding the wind on a topmost branch
Their eyes are only for the main chance,
The dropped chips or unguarded young.
Death's dark companions,
Never happier than when they're beak deep in
    rabbit guts.
Unloved by most – a crow in a cage is no
    ornament,
Their plumage a mere flash of darkness,
And their voices no entertainment,
Just the sound of the rusty hinges of a great
    castle door.
The rumours of their messenger potential
    pure fantasy:
They'd gobble down the message and do a U-
    turn for the corn reward.
In my garden they are pond raiders hunting
    down my hapless frogs.
I flap my arms at them
And skywards they flap,
 Until high above they agitate the sky
 Like the tea leaves in a fortune teller's cup.
 Black boomerangs who will be back.

At the Home

My mother tugs at the neck of the nightdress
which she knows is not her own.
Again.
But today the music is drawing her away.
Ye banks & braes o' bonny Doon...
her voice cracks for a minute
and I take over.
She gives me the look.
I was never the best singer.
But I'm all that she's got.
She resumes the song
tapping out the rhythm
on the faded bedspread
that's trapping her beneath it.
Also not her own.

My mother likes to lie in a bed of roses
patterned like the walls of the faraway
    kitchen,
where her mother sits playing the concertina,
while her sister, who could have been an
    opera singer,
Clarrie of the golden voice,
joins her as she sings:
Thou minds me o'departed joys,
Departed never to return.
The kitchen's cosy with the warmth of the
    range,
the glow of the oil lamps and the family
    pictures.

Her mother stately in a big hat shading her
    eyes,
Clarrie with tinted lips dressed for a concert
    in pearls and velvet.
My mother and little sister all solemn in
    Sunday best.
The kitchen window looks out over the
    orchard
with its drifts of white narcissi, like spring
    snow,
where one day, beneath the bridal wreath
    blossom
of the apple trees,
my Uncle Charlie will come a-courting
    Clarrie
and put an end to her singing career.

My mother is still singing though:
Wi' lightsome heart I pu'd a rose.
She's still by the range in the kitchen
where her memories are her own.
My mother has come home.

David Hurd

Nature's Ways

Little tit, why cough and choke, could it be the
city's smoke?

Coughing tit so weak and frail, in your nest I
see your tail

Poking from your downy bed, the other side of
which your head

Plucks and preens your downy breast to
comfort more your straw bound nest

Little tit I pry nor poke, tell I pray thee, why
you choke?

Tom tit perching just near by flits and flurries
as you cry.

Tell me Tom tit of the cause, I know not of
nature's laws,

Just what ails your feathered wife, what could
cause her grief and strife?

I seem to sense his proud reply "She is with
young, and fathered I.

Formed inside her is an egg, so grieve no more
for her I beg"

Soon the nest has three or more. Pride in which
the father bore

Food and vitals for his spouse, for she cannot
leave the house,

Proud he is to forage for, happy to perform the
chore.

Once or twice throughout the day it is father's
    turn to stay
Home, to keep the family warm, 'til within the
    shell they form.

"Addled", "Coddled" what you say, means it's
    close to hatching day
First the hole and then the split, tumbling to the
    world, a Tit.
First the one and then soon four, eggshell litter
    on the floor.
Helpless, naked, wet and blind, beaks a-gape for
    food to find.
Mother, Father, work in turn, catching food
    amongst the fern.
Grasshopper or common fly, even crumbs of
    cake they ply.
Go to feed their thriving young, for by now has
    summer come.
Parents' labour never stops. Peck for milk
    through bottle tops.
Rummage round for crust of bread. Steal from
    bowl where dog is fed.
Summer now replaces spring. Soon the
    fledglings take to wing.

Their efforts as they try to fly raise parental
    anguish, cry,
    Stumble headlong off the bough. Click!
        Triumphant cat, meow.

Cautious now the other three, frantic flutters
in the tree.
Till at last they learn the art, bold triumphant,
proud at heart.
Round their young the parents sing, offspring
now are on the wing.
Season now is getting late. Soon the swallows
must migrate
Gather, twitter on the wires, as we humans
light our fires.
Once assembled as a flock, of their bearings
they take stock,
Then away to warmer climes, clock of seasons
changes times

Winter takes us in its grip. Snowy pavements
make us slip.
Shiver, freezing in our hose, glowing fires,
chilblains, nose,
Doggedly we stick it out, 'til May is past ne'er
cast a clout.
Tomtits come and sing a song, rendering the
whole day long,

Female makes her homely nest. Male with
male will vie for best.
Champion will female woo, eavesdrop as they
bill and coo.
Tom-tit singing from the bough, I can hear her
coughing now,

I am wise in nature's ways, I know what that
    cough repays.
Though I pity Tom-tit's plight, love from him
    will turn out right.
Soon the egg and then the young, blind and
    naked, weak of lung,
Soon to take their place on high. So patience
    Tom-tit, do not cry.

Winter Snow

Snow is falling, softly snow blankets all the
　　earth below,
Clouds like thunder dark and grim, winter now
　　is setting in.
Now the Yule-tide logs are burned, up are top-
　　coat collars turned,
Feet are shod in fur-lined boots, hungrily the
　　night owl hoots.
Rats across the barn-yard floor hunt for food
　　that he can store,
Near him in his hay loft den, safe retreat from
　　dog and men.
Squirrels in the hollowed oak bushy tails their
　　noses stroke,
Nuts and acorns with them store, so they need
　　not pass the door.

Swifts and swallows all migrate, for they fear
　　the winters hate,
Ravaging their flimsy homes with icy blasts
　　that chill the bones.
Crofters in their lowly shacks fuel for fires
　　never lack,
All the spring he dug for peat and dried it, in
　　the summer's heat.

Softly now the dovecotes sigh for their food they
　　must all fly,
Over hills and fields of white, search for grain
　　or berries bright.
Woods are full of hungry sounds where the
　　rabbit hops and bounds,
Oft you'll hear a choking cry, for the stoat
　　must kill or die.

Trappers with their gin or snare catch them as
    they hunt for fare,
Rabbits cannot store their food, harsh their
    winter, coarse and rude.

The hedgehog in its leafy ball cannot feel the cold
    at all,
Neither can the velvet mole safe and warm
    within its hole,
Birds that squabble for a crust, robins, with
    implicit trust,
Licks its lips a nearby cat, dreams how they
    would make him fat,
Nature with her changing days, teaches us in
    different ways,
Man with knowledge, rudiment still must heed
    the element.

Turnips frozen in the ground, babbling brook
    where is thy sound?
Life is fringed, dormant, still, and will remain
    that way until
Softly, silently, the cold on the earth releases its
    hold,
Warmth will creep into the rays of sunshine, on
    the springtime days.
Till at last the world will thaw, life awaken-
    outwards pour.
Sounds and movement all around, spring is
    sprung with joy abound.
Twitter nibble cough and choke, smell no more
    the peat-fire smoke.

Listen to the babbling brook, see the trees,
  how green they look.
Yes in glory, spring is here, gone is winter
  one more year,
Life to start afresh - amend, till with snow, this
  year will end.

Seasons change

Autumn now is in the air, the season's change
    repeating,
Nature dressed in lush green fare will soon the
    snows be greeting.
The rich green grass soon dries to straw and hugs
    the ground more tightly,
Its growth now halted till the thaw and the sun
    again shines brightly.
The air is nipped, and chill the wind, to slow the
    sap from rising,
The scurrying squirrel acorns find his larder store
    comprising.
For soon he knows the climate change, the cold
    chill wind will bluster,
Far from his nest he must not range so, near his
    food store cluster.

The flow of lifeblood now curtailed, the leaves soon
    start to wither,
To fall and leave the branch revealed, and naked
    limbed to shiver.
The russet rustle as they shed soon carpet the
    forest floor,
With amber, copper, gold and red, and many
    colours more.
The blazoned glory of their hues just takes your
    breath away,
You feel you want to stand and muse and never
    move away.

Hush now, listen, you will hear the seeds of life
    renew,

The crash of conkers, sharp and clear, and
  acorns pattering dew.
The fir trees scaly spiral cone opens wide its
  fronds
Whilst hazel nuts as hard as stone are picked
  when they are bronze.
The holly and the bramble bush grow berries
  shining gay,
As fodder for the Mistle thrush, the Blackbird
  and the Jay.
The hedgehog rustling in the leaves for his final
  meal of worms,
Then rolled beneath the tree root eaves, sleeps
  through the winter storms,

Rabbits thump their warning sound as soon as
  you they see.
Then scurry down beneath the ground until the
  coast is free.
Fledgling rooks from treetop nests now almost
  adult size,
Wheel and glide, dart and jest, on freshening
  winds they rise.
High overhead and southward bound, white
  winged in arrow form,
The swans migrate, their creaking sound
  melodic and forlorn.
Honking arrowheads of geese pursue the
  graceful swan,

They won't return 'til spring release, when
    winter's almost gone.

All creatures wise in nature's ways, prepare to
    face the threat,
That autumn leads to winter days, of cold, and
    dark, and wet.
When rainclouds burst and deluge pour, with
    cold and dampness chill,
By winter time and snow days draw, shorter,
    sharp and shrill,
These autumn days where nature warns, that
    times will worsen yet,
Take heed, the wildlife's different forms prepare
    themselves, get set.

Litter Louts

One hundred, Two hundred, Three hundred yards,
Measure the roadside with large ugly cards,
Printed in black on a background of white,
Enhanced with scarlet, outstanding and bright.

Warnings of risk and of danger of skid.
Above twenty per hour is the risk if you did.
Chippings would fly at the car behind you.
So slow down your speed, do not hasten undue.

Daffodils, bluebells, then dandelions grow
The grass turns to hay as the seasons bestow,
Yet still do remain these road gritting signs.
Their collection has slipped from the contractor's minds.

A fish and chip wrapper or dead cigarette
Could end for me with a fine I could get.
Yet contractors flaunt the no litter code
And abandon their junk at the side of the road.

Just twenty per hour cause the traffic to slow.
Thus tourism buses and work people go.
Delayed in their progress by these cardboard dictates,
Their lack of removal this problem relates.

Give reasonable time for the grit to adhere,
Plus one or two days for the surplus to clear,
Then sweep up the swarf and paint on the lines
Then get the contractors to pick up their signs.

Night

Slowly, silently the night wraps its darkness
   round the light of day
The moon replaces the shimmering glow, weak
   and faint the light it throws,
On earth below, where life lives on, where lovers
   love become as one,
And couples strolling down the lane, for parting
   has such sorrow pain.
The lingering kiss in leafy glade, that, when
   departed kiss will fade,
Later by each bed they kneel for prayer with
   prayer each other feel.
Weep on pillow, parting mourn, sleep will bring
   tomorrow's dawn.
Children in their cot or pen romp in dreamlands,
   heaven, glen.

Cat with whiskers, purrs and sighs, watch the
   embers fade with eyes
Green, fluorescent, burning bright meet the
   challenge of the night.
Rise and stretch and licks its coat, purr no longer
   in its throat.
Night is here, it's pitch as black, still its feline
   sight no lack,

Birds in downy straw bound nest dream on
   eggs or young that blessed,
Nature aid to raise on wing, aid to nature, wing
   raise, sing.
Song so pure and sung so sweet to descant to the
   young lambs bleat.
Patient mothers stand to feed for lamb and calf to
   each its need.

With love so true and tender bring be big or small
   be nature's kin,
For horse and cow in shelter barn with other
   creatures on the farm.
Moon and stars will plough aloft, sleeping
   shepherd, sleeping croft,
Owls to hunting hoot and scan, talons claw at
   mouse that ran,
Frantic scream as claw claw clash, together as for
   hole through dash,
Shiver, panting, quake with fear, up are pointing
   rabbits ear,
Silent, stealthily the stoat, stalk and strike at
   furry throat,
Moonlight whiteness, love and fear, stars that too
   find contrast here.
Barnyard scratching, chick and hen, woodland
   skulking fox lair den,

Some are wakened, some in sleep, some can see the
    faint rays creep,
Silhouette the tree with sky, clouds of scarlet,
    windwards fly.
Night of terror, blissful sleep, waking now, with
    dawn that creep.
Brighter now dawn days that grow, welcome by
    the crow cock's crow,
Stirring, rousing, slumber past, bright bring
    dawn's day, moonlight past.

Stuck

I've broke it, I've bust it, the damn things gone
    kaput,
These accidental happenings just make me do my
    nut!
I'll stick it back together, I'll just find all the bits
Now, where's that tube of what's it - but first I'll
    check it fits.
A squeeze from out the blue tube, and equal from
    the black.
A quick stir with a matchstick, my goodness what
    a stack,
I've got a bit left over, so what else must there be?
Search house and shed and garden, but nothing
    can I see,
The wife says "nothing's broken"; the kids have
    been too good,
There must be something damaged, be it china,
    metal, wood.
I sure as hell can't waste it, that's unforgiven sin,
To screw up the left-overs and chuck 'em in the
    bin.

Blow you

Oh! Sighing, crying wind that flies, invisible
    across the skies,
What moves you?

As summer brings a gentle swell, to waft at
    flowers whilst their smell
Drifts with you.

Corn that stands in fields for drying, and washing
    hung on lines for drying,
Do need you.

A ripple on the quiet stream of moonlight's pale
    fluorescent gleam,
Reflect you.

In summer don't you fill the sail, from helm to
    helm the yachtsmen hail,
Ahoy you.

Thistledown and dandelion, need your whispering
    breeze to fly on,
Spread by you.

Flowers and bushes, of whose seed, is scattered
    far across the mead,
Do thank you.

Alone you cause the leaves to fall, to huddle
 close, against the wall,
What chills you?

Tides that roll in, wave on wave, which seamen
 sniff in manner grave,
Predict you.

Transforms the summer's fleecy cloud then
 autumn makes us ask aloud
What ails you?

Anger rage and turmoil run from skies so dark
 they hide the sun,
Men fear you.

Why dark in daylight heaven's cloud, with flash
 of light and thunder loud,
Arraign you.

In winter don't you bring the snow to blanket
 grip the earth below?
Freeze with you.

Seasons change like day to night fickle wind
 from storm to light,
Who rules you?

Gentle whisper barely sighing kiss the cheek of
    baby crying,
God bless you.

Life you touch in every phase, some will hate you
    some will praise
God for you.

Oh! Sighing crying wind that fly to push the
    clouds across the sky,
Blow, oh blow you.

Child's Prayer

Please Jesus teach me to be good,
To do the things a good boy should,
To love my Mammy and my Dad,
To help all people to be glad,
To say my prayers to you each day,
Help me Jesus, Help I pray.

Training by Sgt D Hurd RE

When I rush out to "Stand To" with my gas mask
    and me gun,
I think about me father who said, "you'll rue it
    son".
But I was thick and stupid, and didn't give a cuss,
You see, I was a big-'ead who thought he knew it,
    bust.
When I got into khaki, I met a little squirt,
This little sod called Chalky, just rubbed me in
    the dirt.
He screamed and raved and ranted at me, when
    e'er we met,
He very near got planted, I'll get that bastard, yet.
But I've been in the Army, for many many years,
'Midst bullies, squealers, good guys and some who
    bring me tears.

Now I'm in charge of training, to teach the
    "sprogs" the ropes,
I'll drill, and rant and badger, and save his life,
    one hopes.
To make a decent squaddy you need to make him
    hate!
It's you, it's them, it's someone's, it's someone
    else's fate.
Now I hate little Chalky, I have and always will,
But that wee runt has taught me, to war, to stalk,
    to kill

But now I know my duty, to hold, with all my
    might,
This land, for Queen and country, for freedom
    and for right.
For here I'm free to tell you just what I think
    and feel,
That democratic teaching which makes our
    freedom real.
It's something the world envies, I'm British, and
    I'm proud,
And no-one, even Hitler, was able to enshroud.
Because of little Chalky, the lessons he taught
    me,
And I have taught to others, we're British and
    we're free.

Futility 1 Sept 1991

My dearest love please to watch over
This shell of a man left behind.
Be with me in deed and at times when I need
You to bolster my heart, and my mind.
How I miss you, I just can't engender.
Things we should have, together attained.
Gone our love Oh so precious, so tender.
It's the why that cannot be explained.

It's so wrong to be here now without you.
It's so hard to find reasons to live.
So unfair of the cancer that took you
When we still had a lifetime to give.
Alone I'm so brim full of memories.
Their reason has frittered and died,
And I wake, to find tears on my pillow,
To find that's another night cried.

Charlie Bains

A heap of bones, a pile of stones, 'tis all remains
  of Charlie Bains,
This tartan shirt amongst the dirt, it's faded hue
  too old to sew.
It's laid there long, but it was strong, it had to be,
  it covered he.
He wore it rolled through sweat or cold, his arms
  expose such arms as those,
Should never be, for they made three of any man,
  who dared to stand,
In front of him, for with his grin the world would
  quake, for he could break,
The back of any, as he had many a pup, who
  thought his legend nought.

One hand would take, to hold and shake, till on
  his knee big men would plea.
His hands so big with them to dig, with twelve
  inch span would wash and pan,
To wrestle with dirt, with death to flirt, to keep his
  stream, to hunt a gleam,
A little glow, the one you know, to drive men mad
  as Charlie had.
His whole life long he knew one song, a voice
  would crow, a shrill "Strike Oh"
Then Hell would split and crack and spit, and
  man would fight with man for right
To dig and scratch, or steal and snatch, the life of
  one the wife of one.

Rape and rampage, this bloody age, of rampant
    beasts and drunken feasts,
Where life was cheap and women weep, where
    men would die and children cry.
Good men would work where bad ones lurk, to
    jump their claim, 'midst rifle rain.
Yet in this lot a little tot, became a boy, his
    father's joy.
To grow a man, where life began, this hardy life
    amongst the strife.
Here in the wood he often stood, for days be there,
    to stand aware,
Of natures play throughout the day, and of her
    fight throughout the night.

Of life and death in every breath, did train him
    hard, his life to guard.
Now, as a man, no one could ban, for where he go,
    no man would show,
That he was wrong, or not yet strong, enough to
    match, this rugged batch.
Men from the east more like the beast those from
    the south were far less couth.
But Charlie grew amongst that crew, where, what
    you get is what you got,
For many a year, to curse and swear, and then to
    find that life was kind.
That day among the hills a long, and gusty shout,
    did summon out,

"Strike Oh, Strike Oh", did Charlie go. Ye gods the
   bellow and see the Yellow.

It's all around, this Charlie found, he made his
   name, his fame.
He ran it rich within that pitch, the stuff he found
   beneath the ground,
Was good and pure, and rich for sure. This
   Charlie won his life begun.
He drank a lot, and even shot, a man, a pup that
   rubbed him up,
But always just, he had no trust, in fellow man,
   this gift of pan.
Was his for keeps, for as he sleeps he's half awake
   in case they take
The slightest chance of moonlight dance, to wrest
   his gold from out his hold.

He held it tight by day or night, sober or drunk
   ne'er lost a chunk.
This power of wealth and vibrant health obsessed
   with gain he felt no pain.
For more he strove himself he drove, to reach and
   clasp all in his grasp.
Until at last, he met his match, She lured him on
   till all was gone.
The fire within his fearful grin, flickered and died
   just like his pride,
To beg her back he'd dog her track, he'd pray,
   he'd plead, she paid no heed,

A broken man, a rusty pan, a mug, a plate, a
    kick of fate
Great was his stand against the land, but paid
    the toll, she took his all.
She dulled his flame, her slave became, just with
    her grin she mastered him,
Then drove her slave to an early grave, a heap of
    dust a hollow crust,
An empty shell to rest in hell, that tartan shirt
    there in the dirt.
Did once look fine, was it not mine?
This heap of bones, that pile of stones,
    Are not remains of Charlie Bains.

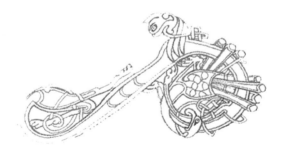

Orderly Telephone

I've got a new pen, now what can I write? I've got
to do something to fill in the night.
For here I am lumbered on duty T.O. unless I do
something the time doesn't go.
So here I sits ponderin', a-thinking a-might, tryin'
to compile me some nonesense to write,
I sits here a-smokin' an' nursin' a frown, I thinks
Oh so hard, but I can't get it down,
To paper, a record of thoughts I may keep, already
I've lost over half a night's sleep.

A subject, I want one I know lots about, well
would you believe it, I can't think of owt.
I could tell a tale all sordid and grim, well be
quick about it the lights going dim,
Or like that bloke Hans I could tell a rhyme I
would if I could but I just ain't got time,
To sit here bemoaning the fate that befell young
Hansel and Gretel in that grotty dell.

Of history too I know nowt about, cept 'Enery the
eighth an 'e were a lout,
Agreed he got married again and again, other than
that I know nowt of 'is reign.
Of Cavaliers, Roundheads, ten sixty six, even Guy
Fawkes who made bombs just for kicks,
I envy them folks who reel it off pat, it must be
pure sawdust what's under me hat.

Of sports I could prattle but what can I say, I
    don't even watch it now let alone play.
Sometimes play Rugby, but that's just for fun, if I
    got the ball now I can't even run,
The object behind it to try anyhow, to carry this
    pumpkin surrounded by cow,
From halfway or centre to twenty feet past, or hit
    the man trying, before it gets passed.

Played by all big men 'airy and fick, you belt 'im or
    try to before 'e can kick,
Over the meadows you follow it far, well blow that
    for luck mate it's over the bar.
Hockey, the same sort of object or goal, twenty
    men golfing, not one ruddy hole,
They belt at that little white ball with a stick, then
    if they don't hit it they give it kick.

Tried cricket, Oh blimey, how daft can you be?
    They point at three sticks now 'ere's half a tree,
Now I get back here, and aim with this ball, you've
    got t'hit it or they twigs will fall,
Then you is out, but mate that's not half, you've
    got two big mattresses strapped to your calf,
Now hit the ball low 'cause if it goes high they
    catch it an keep it an "Owzat" they cry,
Up with thy bat and homewards you plod, it's
    miles from out yonder, back over t' sod.

Tennis and badminton, almost the same, they
   used to be once 'til a bird changed the name.
There's tennis on tables or cupboards and chairs,
   that is until Mum finds out God how she
   swears.
From here we digress to aquatic stints where
   Weissmuller's Tarzan could pick up some hints,
To dive from so high in swallow or pike, a feeling
   unnerving god knows what it's like.
To stand on a springboard and lurch into space
   but if you misjudge, it's a hospital case.

Some swim like a fish with barely a splash, I tried
   it myself once, did I make a hash.
Enough said of sport I fear that must be, a new
   trend of thought has just come to me,
I must stop for a smoke or even a rest for poor as
   it is I'm trying my best,
To join all my thoughts in logical line, on reading
   back through it, ain't I doing fine?

I could write some more but let's not I think, I'll
   climb in me pit now, in sleep I will sink,
One, two, three up to eight, that crafty wee
   blighter went under the gate,
My dreams they do wander, free they do soar, how
   peaceful my slumbers oh! blast must I snore,
The telephone rings with its shrill piercing cry
   "Orderly Telephone can I help you?" I sigh.

Ruth Kershaw

The empty nest – Sidcup

It was lonely when the girls left home;
We're proud of them, they've done well.
But of course, we brought them up proper.
So they would, wouldn't they?
We have the house to ourselves now.
Haha, a right 'Darby and Joan' me and Bert are.
Free to take holidays on our own –
Though I always like to get back to our little bungalow.
We live in a very good part of town.

But I do miss Lily and Joyce.
They wanted more than this, more life, they said,
And off they shot, Lily first at seventeen
(she's married now of course.
They come to visit occasionally).
Then Joyce went two years later – hairdressing –
We don't see much of her.
Footloose and fancy free. You know.

Well, we went to the Isle of Wight last year
And here's this couple from up North,
Like us in many ways; respectable.
They just had one girl.
She was away from home too,
Early twenties, a student.
And you'd never have guessed,
She was coming here on a course.

'We'll have her,' Bert said,
'It'll be company for Daisy
And save the girl looking for digs.
We're only a mile from college.'

And so Joan arrived 'fait accompli'
As they say. She was nice enough
But it was kind of awkward.
We are always in bed early
And some days she had lectures 'til nine.
And we had to ask her not to bang the door
When she got in. But then we'd hear her
Splashing about in the bathroom.
But the thing that really got me was her accent,
From the North, you know.

Lancashire of all places!
Well I found it grating, of course.
One day I said to her,
'Joan, however did you get into a Grammar School
With such a strong Northern accent?'
She didn't hesitate;
'I went to a Northern Grammar School,'
She came back.
'Ooher!' I said.
Soon after that, she found other digs –
Nearer to the College, she said,
With a young couple that had a baby.
They hoped she would sit for her sometimes.
Maybe she fitted in better there.
She only came back once to see us.

No, we didn't take anyone else in..
Maybe Lily will start a family.
It would be nice to have a grandchild.
No, we don't see much of them.
But we enjoy our holidays, of course,
And meet up with some very nice people.

Out of context

Waiting in the bus station
The bearded man ahead
Smiled and said, 'Hello.'
I knew him well,
Returned the smile.
Not seen him here before!

Who was he??
Searched the alphabet
To try and catch his name
J. John.. John who?

The bus came in.
He headed for the back.
I chose front... thinking.
Memory there.
Dig deeper.

John – of course, Pam's husband:
Pam the friend, but
We had been to their house.
They had dined with us.

Bus still standing.
I hurried to the back.'
'It's John!' I said.
'Yes' – big smile.

Then, 'who are you?'

The Helm Wind

Our only named wind – Capital H
The Helm
Blasts the Eden Valley from Crossfell

Crossfell. Highest of the Pennine Chain,
Renamed.
Once Fiends Fell until
St Augustine exorcised the resident demons and
scattered them lower down.
The Cross then erected on the summit.

The Helm is formed by an encounter.
Cold air from the east meets warmer air from the West
Forming a cap of helm cloud.
This bar rises
parallel to the skyline then
rotates

A ferocious gust
Rushes down.
Branches whirl,
Men stagger,
It is even said it can blow
The nebs off the geese.

Hunker down
Do not risk your kite!

RESCUE FROM THE BATHTUB   -
Distressed ballad.

Blistering SHINGLES is an itchy thing –
You lose a lot of sleep –
The fifth night in, I ran a bath
Of water, warm and deep.

The luxury of lying there,
Sheer bliss without a doubt,
I soaked and soaked; then, mortified,
Found I could not get out!

Impossible for David too
But he knew who to phone.
Help on the way…
But was there time to cover bone?

In gold pyjamas, bath now dry,
I greeted them (no longer bare),
The men in green with gloves of blue
When they bounded up the stair.

Youngsters they seemed to me,
But sturdy both and strong.
`Can I get into the bath with you?'
Said one, `It shouldn't take too long.'

`Feel free', said I (for never before
Had I had a chance like this),
Chucking something in behind me,
He clambered in – not much amiss.

He lifted me, then passed me to his mate
Who sat me on the toilet lid
To take blood pressure and more
Which soon he did.

So, all was well, they went
Much too polite for snickers.
I grabbed the black thing from the bath –
He'd been standing on my knickers!

And now I'm aching from the struggle -
Like having lost a fight.
I'll fix a grab rail on the wall.
Next time I'll be all right.

John S Langley

The Pen

The pen is but a pen
a tool to be guided
across a virgin landscape
of bleached, pressed, pulped wood

The pen does not think
of what it writes
the meaning of the marks
it leaves behind
It has no memory
no conscience
no reason to act
or not to act

It is the hand
that wields the pen
that shapes scratches
that magically share
meaning

and leave a trace
A pathway from the past
a message to the future
by way of now
The pen is but a pen

Time to Tread Water

We have three sons
and if there was a time
for the clocks to stop
for time to freeze
then it was when
they were 7, 9 and 10 years old

Time could have decided
to tread water
keeping us afloat
but no more

Time to Repeat

When every day was full
of learning and the fun
of new discoveries
for them
and for us

Repeating the Times

When holidays were spent in tents
in France
Buying oysters by the bucket
and fresh bread
as long as your arm

And when

Money was tight
every penny counted
from pay check to pay check
with a Mortgage around our neck
like an albatross

And

when there was playing, and laughing
falling, and crying
all in a rush
Making cakes in a mess
Boiling eggs and toasting soldiers

To Repeat
and loop
through the good
and the not so good
until there was no more time

and we stood together
and watched
as the Moon bled away
shimmering
into the sea

But what am I thinking!

These are my wishes
not theirs

They wanted to grow
they wanted to go
on their own journeys

and I could not
take that away from them
even if time
had made the offer

I guess that's what love is
I guess that's what time does

Marsden Rocks

Tidal caves to explore
with stone worn sea swell smooth
that echoes to the sounds of running feet
of pirates, smugglers, and highwaymen
and their watchful Mothers

And after them the crashing sea
rises in white salty fountains of spray
the diurnal wind driven tides
rush and return again and again
dancing in time to the Moon

A young boy's belief in the everlasting
nature of standing stone
is shattered in the noise
of crashing waves
of broken stone
and the collapsing arch

that was supposed to stand
as a sentry to anchored memory
A rock amidst swirling seas
a buttress for a returning prodigal
searching for the stability of home

Now the new view is home
to new feet that skirt the surf
around the Marsden Rocks
to pirates, smugglers and highwaymen
and their watchful Mothers

Running through the Days

Running through the days
at a breakneck speed
that is too slow
to match the pace
of new things passing
one after the other

Running through the days
of schooled lessons
that drip away the clock
between bell rung playtimes
full of friendships and feuds
one after the other

Running through the days
that stop you in your tracks
as fresh eyes hook you
into an awakening
the chiming, breaking, healing of hearts
one after the other

Running through the days
with a growing strength
that seeks a purpose
to tie to beliefs
in other people's battles
one after the other

Running through the days
at the distinguished pace
of acquired knowledge
and the worldly-wise
filled with life's lessons
one after the other

Running through the days
watching as new tricks pass
and you steam
in the age of electricity
crackling out discharged tales
one after the other

Running through the days
at the speed of memory
when the days go slowly
and the years race
and the sunsets pass
one after the other

Running
Running
Through the days ...

Tell me a story about 3 things

Tell me a story about 3 things
A pirate, a boat and a bat
a policeman in a top hat
Then I'll go to sleep
I promise

Tell me a story about 3 things
A girl, a boy and a broken heart
A way to get back to the start
Then I'll smile again
I promise

Tell me a story about 3 things
A bard, a laugh and a snake
The mistakes I'd better not make
I might listen this time
I promise

I'll tell you a story about 3 things
A mountain, a man and a goat
The memories that keep us afloat

If you don't go to sleep
you promise

If there is a time

If there is a time
when I don't recognise you
when I don't recognise your face
Don't cry
It's not what I wanted either

If there is a time
when you look into my eyes
and I'm no longer there
Don't cry
I didn't do it on purpose

If there is a time
when you remember me like that
then do it without guilt and
Don't cry
I don't want to be remembered that way

If there is a time
When you think of me as I was
when days were brighter
Then smile
Don't cry
and in your heart I'll smile back

Conversations with Grief

Hello, said Grief
Oh hello, I said
I'm just here to find out
how things are going
They're horrible, I said
Oh good, said Grief
Would you like me to go?
I would really like you to go
Then I'll stay, said Grief
settling down in a favourite chair

Hi, said Grief
Hi, I said
I thought I'd give you a surprise
It's been a while
Not very long at all, I said
I just wanted to make sure, said Grief
that you hadn't forgotten about me
Oh, I haven't forgotten
That's good, said Grief, I'll be here to remind
you
Would you like me to go?
Would you listen? I said
Of course not, said Grief
taking out an old memory

What's up, said Grief
What's up, I said
 I'm back again
 Can't keep me away
That's OK, I said, I'm getting used to it
 I think I'll stick around for a bit, said Grief
 Would you like me to go?
You do what you want, I said
I think we need to learn
how to get along.

St. Mary's Island

Jellyfish are stranded upon the sand
star struck in surprise

Hermit crabs swap houses
mortgage free in rock pools

Dry shells are collected, sorted, glued
to be reborn as souvenirs

more wholesome than the postcards
that shout out their saucy messages
in primary colours

And tidally approachable
stands the extinguished lighthouse
like an unlaunched Saturn V rocket
staring upwards at unexplored spaces

Gulls cry against the quieting shush
of the shingle
crashing waves lift the taste of salt
into the air
to meet cold noses, open mouths
and bare arms tickled by the sea's breeze

Here is the world around St Mary's Lighthouse
where the light flickers in the changing tides

where the causeway deepens then clears
deepens then clears
as the tides turn

Argumentative

There was not a day
when we did not argue
You said it helped with the circulation
but I begged to differ

We could not even agree
where the borderline was
between a disagreement
and an argument

The words would fall sharply
but mercifully quick
making space for the next
falling out

What did we argue about?
You know, I can't remember

So many little things
that did not matter

Not so many big things
We were too engrossed in coping
to argue about those

And now

I have so many little things
I want to argue with you about
but can't

I miss that

I miss not being able to disagree with you
at least three times a day
for the good of my circulation

How dare you leave me alone
before I'd finished arguing

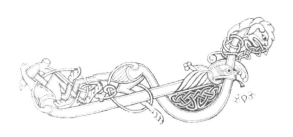

Finding a way down

Take a step, take a next step
onto mountain, bog and heath
worrying less about what lies underneath
than finding your own way down, and back
as the mist descends silently and you tack
that way and this to manage the slope
hidden in white and you only hope
that the earlier jest that 'you should take a rope'
doesn't hang you instead in the blindness
of these fells

Timeless and tied together when they turn
in a shapeless world of damp trickle-down
when a warm hand and a friendly face
is all you desire to replace the rising fear
of going nowhere and reaching nowhere
but doing it fast

then through fogged and dewy eyes you
see the white becoming brighter and whispering away
as fast as it came and you're left sodden and still
and seeing now that the Car Park is just there
 solid as a rock

and you smile and you stare promising yourself
you will never be this foolish again, knowing
that you will when the memory has warmed
into a good story and you walk to the car
and hang on to its welcome

and remember the way to the pub
and that this place is a hard place to call home
But then again all places are hard places
to call home

Stuart Turner

In Praise of the Country

My heart is in the country
In its greenness, life and smells
In shaded copse on meadows gay
And in its secret sylvan dells

My heart is in the country
Where finch and lapwing play
Where cattle low and ploughshare turns
Many furrows from the clay

My heart is in the country
By its weathered farmhouse door
Its barns and swooping swallows
In hot sun or winter hoar

My heart is in the country
In the olden church's pews
Where echoes of the past live on
In the shade of ancient yews

My heart is in the country
Where the honest labourers toil
Sowing, tending and reaping crops
From the good earth's fertile toil

My heart is in the country
In its measured peaceful ways
Round its sparkling streams and fields
Where the boxing hare still plays

My heart is in the country
Where our maker and man unite
'Mid flowers, bees and birds
In its peace, its sheer delight

My heart is in the country
In the cottage or grandest hall
Where God is round each corner
Of forest, field and wall

My heart is in the country
In its serene unaltered way
Forever a green and pleasant land
Forever here to stay

The Pendragon Spell

I had searched to find the seat
Of Uther Pendragon's clan
This autumn it lay before me
Ruined, forbidding and wan.

The grey stones echoed eerily
As I stood at the gaping door
And a raven black in feather and eye
Stared down at me as of yore.

The bird lifted into the air
From the ruined castle wall.
It fixed me with a backward glance
And I heard the dead ones call.

I followed the bird when it beckoned
And steered off towards the west
Its wings beat slow and steady
Ever onwards without rest.

To the setting sun flew the raven
As the valley gulped the night
And the high hills reared to void
Where a star hung diamond bright.

No noise came o'er the stillness
Save the chilling breezes' tones
As above an owl at its quarter
As the mist slithered over the stones.

Onward still flew the raven
A speck in the lonely glare
Forever etched on my mind
I could only stand and stare.

More stars came out from their hiding,
A moth came fluttering free,
The uplands nodding off to sleep
And no one there but me.

Then the owl it hooted farewell,
The raven had flown from sight
More stars shone as the darkness closed
I stood alone in the velvet night.

Was it the ghost of a wizard
I had followed on moor and fell?
Or was it just the spirit of place
Which had held me in its spell?

Death of a Fox

I

I wandered silently
it seemed
along the paths of Pan
and dreamed that merry wood-nymphs danced
and in my veins the ichor ran.

Contentment lulled in
the drowsy breast
of rural field and the furrow, but
as yet unknown
the poetry of life behest
all with a silver sorrow.

II

No finer day had ever donned
such rich attire as I strolled on
contemplating this and that, and where and
   what
and how and when and why the bee
in his parlour sat
sipping at his ease the nectar of early Autumn
   blooms
while his fragile symbion,

the trusting Painted Lady
fluttered too & fro a little jealous.
A bright eyed squirrel
cheeks apuff with fruit of the field

studied me with unshaken stare, wondering,
then returned to the urgent task of living
in the bowels of an old oak, arms outflung
in appreciation, yet strangely like a crucifix,
leafy offerings at her feet.

Peace enclosed in all without, within
lay heavy, gazed on by the moon waiting on her
invisible shelf, one eye on Phoebus's fiery chariot
blazing low towards the West, seeking
scented breezes and the cricket's chirp.
Across the hill, in some unfettered hollow
a summoning curfew tolled,
and at my feet, sure in military step,
a patrol of ants were about on some
communal quest, dwarfed

in the chaotic jungle grandeur
of the cornfield's edge.
Beside a warbling stream,
uttering notes unheard in Carmen or Die Fliedermaus
a willow hung its saddened head and wept.
"For what?" I asked aloud of it.
The sea of wheat, for mice and men
and other micro-multitudes, the staff of life,
stood strange, a million sun drenched ears
were leaning in the wind, attentive, listening.
I too listened.
I also heard.
Away, as yet unseen, the play was being
enacted, a common enough gesture of

man's eternal misbehaviour.
Was I witness to yet another bloody deed?
The urgent, condemned yelping came
stealthily on, echo'd on its heels by
the other sound, fearful in its cruel ascent,
of baying hounds, the animal tools of man.

I slowly shuddered.
the air had flopped onto its haunches,
still as the frosted grave, no birds sang now,
instead they waited restlessly
on many a woodland branch, in troubled rows
the woodlark, thrush and rook so staunch
preening coats in readiness and
central in the field, alone, even the scarecrow
ankle deep in soil stood withdrawn,
face aghast, eyes sunk black in deep remorse,
regret, I realised of course he'd seen it all
before, unlike myself.
I know not what entranced me, what
made me mortal from my fancied flight,
but stay I knew I must.
Quick as sand, a movement caught my eye
There on the far bank, sculptured like a bronze,
stood the sleek russet form of the hunted,
and hunted well he looked.
pausing saving seconds, eyes darted
like black diamonds weighing up the form,
then cobra-like in slinking dignity
plunged through the effacing stream
into the gold haven beyond, strategy unfurled.

Torment, the other player on this
careering stage, came flooding over the hill
ears a'cock, loins pulsing in inherited
primeval lust, although it seemed
for an instant, painful in its sojourn
the instruments of death might yet be
cheated of their prey but: Alas!
in the form of a mounted black and
scarlet Talisman the force of destiny
played its hand.
I feared his departure from this world,
with all its rending flesh and crunching bones.
What futile purpose would it serve?
Is this the way of sport for pleasing kings and urban
    crones?
the pack, however, heard not my mind-lipped
prayer, just leaped the intervening abyss
in full cry,
eager for the gnashing, rampant kill.
Nature held its breath, perhaps expected more,
but Reynard, wearied of the chase,
was equal to his fate, for deliberately
as if he knew the world were watching,
broke the coercive air,
thrusting his snout in anger to the heavens.
His furry mask glanced my way, asking,
nay pleading, for forgiveness in his degradation,
    his final hour.
How magnificent was that countenance.
Bitterness, pride, burnished defiance
panicked o'er that profile as he viewed his last,
    and barking chided –

"Farewell my rustic friends
forget not my sacrifice
your life is spared because of this."
A strangled howl, long and searching,

issued from his tired upturned throat,
the ancient laws of life (and death),
crossed the Vulpine mind I'm sure,
and in that shrilling cry he seemed to ask
"My god, why have you forsaken me?"
then he died, horribly.

III

A blushing wren began to sing
A violet laid its head
A cortege of rooks took to the wing
The country mourned its dead.

A sighing wind blew from its heart
 a worm writhed in the clay
A spirit wailed to depart
And Earth resumed her crowded day.

The Haaf Netter

The fickle Solway tides have ebbed
 and flowed for millennia
now, chest deep in the incoming water
the fisherman selects his spot
feet set, muscles tense, his form
picked out by a halo of diffused light

Statuesque, like another expert, the heron,
He goes about his work;
no need here for EU supervision and quotas
he sways in the swirling onrush
looking almost as if he's about to be drowned.

On the wilder parts of the shore
speckled clusters of pink and yellow
flicker in the salted air as
groups of dunlin and sandpiper trot
busily intent on their own catch.

Later as sea light fades
and shorebound sounds echo in
the gathering stillness
the haaf netter wades ashore
encumbered but carrying two salmon.

Silhouetted against the dying western sky
an ancient sight is relived
man and nature intertwined
and though nature is vast, the sky interminable
man has his place too.

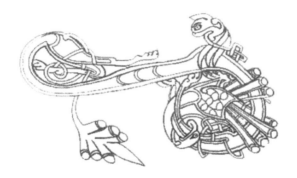

Evening at Brampton

St Martin's bells the hours call
And quickly now the shadows creep
Around the cottage wall

The wood and copse are deathly still
As twilight falls there is no sound
Save for the blackbird's trill

Even the byre is hushed within
A few late swallows swoop above
Their supper meal to win

On zephyr breeze the barn owls glide
And stealthy heron haunts the stream
In nooks the field mice hide

From Solway side the gold clouds steal
Yon darkling rooks head home to roost
Round eaves the first bats wheel

The chariot sun slips off his perch
One blazing arc of molten red
On fire a silver birch

The day is spent, the moon a guest
Finds earth's great tumult stilled
As man and nature rest.

Tuesday 4.30.am.

As if I needed more
encouragement
I wake to satisfy
some nocturnal urge, and see
the night evaporate
to rested day,
sparrows sing a roundelay.
Warm beside me
one rose sleeps,

below, another stirs and wakes
all in a kidnapped hour,
of peace.

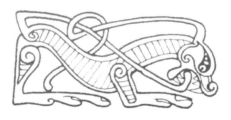

Glimpse

Waiting to turn right
I noticed, through a broken
fence, a field of buttercups
surround a ruffled pond.
A square eye of teasing beauty
gripped by industry,
laughing at its
inevitable fate.

Seconds

A few see death
a few see birth
a few see journeys
dance in drifting mirth

A few see faults
a few see worth
but all in shoals together
scour the restless earth

A few see War
a few see peace
a few seem wistful that
their time will never cease.

Lanercost in Summer Rain

Damply dripping branches
Sinister in the shadow light
As the river rushes seaward
Bearing unknown cargo

Ghosts of Romans, Saxons
And even monks
Watch us as we skip stones
Over deeply shelving pools.

This is July
But more like autumn
With streaming, slate grey clouds
Horizons bounded, weeping.

For whom do they weep?
Those already departed
Or for today's people blundering on
Simultaneously careworn, careless

Cracked stones stand mute
Immured in the silty edges of river bed
They know much
But are silent, reluctant.

I feel a shiver, cold
Feather down my back
It is an eerie, solemn place this
Full of memory and menace.

Even the passing endless seconds
Cannot match the relentless patter
Of a million raindrops
Wetly preening the landscape,
Washing history.

Romany Carol

Lord, the dark and weeping sky
On a Sunday in December
Sleet and snow and horse and dog
In the country I remember

Lord love and preserve us
We pray you this night

Not the tiny Christ child
Rocking in the cradle
Nor the sacred choirs of angels
Singing carols round the gable

Lord love and preserve us
We pray you this night

No shimmering guiding star
Winking through the cloudy glass
Nor even the wise men kneeling
Before the haloed holy lass

Lord love and preserve us
We pray you this night

Just a simple ancient vardo
On a frozen roadside verge
Just humble travellers sheltering
Against the winter's snowy surge

Lord love and preserve us
We pray you this night

Thank you for buying this Anthology

Now here is some space for you to add some poems of your own

Poetry Anthology

Brampton Poets 2019

Lightning Source UK Ltd.
Milton Keynes UK
UKHW011805051019
351070UK00001B/4/P

9 781999 667641